# Them That Slept

# Them That Slept

NEW & SELECTED POEMS

*Larissa Szporluk*

TUPELO PRESS

T P

Them That Slept



Library of Congress Control Number: 2026012940
Cataloging-in-Publication Data available upon request.
ISBN: 978-1-961209-67-1 (paper), 978-1-961209-73-2 (eBook)

Cover and text design by adam b. bohannon.
Cover art: Giuseppe Sammartino (1720-1793), *Cristo Velato*, 1753.
Capella Sansevero, Naples, Italy


First paperback edition September 2026



Tupelo Press
P.O. Box 1767
North Adams, Massachusetts 01247
(413) 664-9611 / Fax: (413) 664-9711
editor@tupelopress.org / www.tupelopress.org

Tupelo Press is an award-winning independent literary press that publishes fine fiction, non-fiction, and poetry in books that are a joy to hold as well as read. Tupelo Press is a registered 501(c)(3) nonprofit organization, and we rely on public support to carry out our mission of publishing extraordinary work that may be outside the realm of the large commercial publishers. Financial donations are welcome and are tax deductible.

*But now is Christ risen from the dead,*
and *become the first-fruits of them that slept.*

(I. CORINTHIANS, 15.20)

# CONTENTS

## I.

(from *Dark Sky Question*, 1998)


Sanctuary 3
Ignis Fatuus 4
Flight of the Mice 6
Radiolaria 7
Io Remembers 9
Holy Ghost 10
Duressor 12
Solar Wind 13
Benefits of Drowning 15
Koan 16
Eel 18


## II.

(from *Isolato*, 2000)


One Thousand Bullfrogs Rejoice 21
Leaving the Eccentric 22
Isolato 24
Givers and Takers 25
Homogeny 27
Meteor 28
Elsewhere 29
Deer Crossing the Sea 31

## III.

(from *Embryos and Idiots*, 2007)


[Argument] 35
Boulders 36
Idol 37
Pornography 38
Reaper 39
Ignoramus 40
Passive-Aggressive Music 41
Naves and Navels 42
Weavers 43
Accessory 44
Stalactite Habit 45
S.O.S 46
Transubstantiation 48
Pecuniary 49
Victorious Female 51
Dark Eros 53
I, Anoton 54


## IV.

(from *The Wind, Master Cherry, the Wind*, 2003,
*Traffic with Macbeth*, 2011, and *Virginals*, 2021)


Circling Disease 59
Fruit of Discord 60
Mangiafuoco 61
Ladybirds 62
Sunflower 63
Windmill 64
Water Bears 66
Tantalus Gossips 67

Rooster's Greeting 68
Claw Asteroid 70
Virginals 71
Trance Logic 73
Dinnerbird 75
Murder-Music 77
Frost 79
Surrender to the Maid 80

## V.
New Poems

Farm before Time 85
L-Field 86
Abel 88
Peacock Mosaic 89
Remanence 90
Moss 92
Yam House 93
Triple Crime 95

# I.

## Sanctuary

Who loves the world? The sleeper does.
Where he is, the jungle is still large.
The things that sing, sing flight into his heart,
and sky, and sun, and sounds so glad
he thinks his mother was a bird,
but singing, warn him, as she didn't,
of the scourge to come, and feed him,
not as she did, warm against her plumes,
thistles, moths, and worms,
but a hundred false beginnings
so the true one will be watered down,
will barely hurt him, scourge,
the true one, whose coming will ignite
like Babylon the Great, in whose hold
he'll perish like a river in a cherished bed,
slowly turning pebbles, tossing mud
and weed, and fling himself
at last, like parrots leaving trees
for cages made of brass, too fresh and green,
too real once, to dream of real things.

## Ignis Fatuus

I can't cope in the bog light.
I was made big and not great.

Moths swarmed in from the plains,
wings of all sizes.

And to think that I did the same,
half-cry of a star

whose boundaries were torn,
then your special way of walking

on the peels. Beautiful voiceless things
were boiled alive.

For three thousand days, I asked you
to stop it.

Little girls are scarcer now.
There won't be a second bride.

Who could go on trying?
Victims form a line even God doesn't know,

their desire for home
snuffed out like a phantom.

I’ll catch silk in the night wind instead,
narrations of our baby.

Part of the sky is all of the sky.
The rest is wasted.

## Flight of the Mice

It was a small dream, like our dream,
built on the small wish to be home
once the home had been broken,
leveled by misunderstanding, by dodging,
by the loud brunt of dark, and it broke
all the plans and the ferns and soft earth
they had known, so they ran for the end
of the grasses, as you ran out of threats,
your voice a torn wire fence without land
to enclose, a disobeyed boundary,
shaking to remember where it had owned.
No one sees what they need to survive.
No one sees the dream thicken and rise
like the old foundation, the pieces of life
that were good, that stood the strong weather,
the one with the other, us, inside,
that intrudes on you now as you reach
what they reached, a waste as effaced as the sky,
their eyes overworked with their fabulous
loss, concrete as the race against time.

## Radiolaria

Maybe the earth where her house is
is dangerous,
the foundation easing away.

Maybe alone, in the husk,
she's more of herself, less unsafe.
Bereavement means travel,

nearly, a plane with no wings,
her face on the rug…
*But I asked him to leave,*

*he was stretching…*
Slush in the lowlands.
It must have been an old

attachment. Something
outside of her is thinking,
*I didn't even feel him;*

she was drawn down.
Her vowels went dark.
Her body rowed back

to a time when loss
was not yet architecture,
but still on the eyes

as the weight that would make
her want to build,
when rocks opened up,

and small lives within,
and within, opened up,
until their skins filled the water,

and rose to the sun-realm.
Maybe she rose with them,
and landed here, as they flew on,

and like their broken skeletons,
she's staying flat
to grow elaborate again.

## Io Remembers

There is no sound at all on this wild upland.
The horses have stopped falling
in their great arc through the air.
The panic that carried their necks over the crag
became, early on, in their legs, regret.
The dark knowing that spoils the morning
enters them now, showing them how,
like a difference in contour, they weren't the real
power of the field. How their bearing was minor,
their bones meaning more to the earth
than what each aloof mane in the wind had been.
Their eyes, which before were clear, crowd
with the fleas madness brings, as she notes
in the noonday heat how each part lies,
spread across rock, like her own in that scene,
half-girl, half-cow, the cloud half-off.

# Holy Ghost

All my thoughts of you are good ones.
*The horse whose neck is clothed with thunder—*
they are good ones.
*The voice that shakes the wilderness*—good ones.
I think about how, if I could wake up,
I could go to your life,
how that would be good, if I could wake up.

But where I am is so large.
You are a fly.
You are impossible.

Where I am is so large, like a dark saying,
repeating. Where I am
is repeating. I don't know where it begins.

Where I am is the same,
but the light just takes you away, and I
am the only one here.
It's mine, like a dark saying—
*Hide them in the dust together.*

*Bind their faces in secret.*
You see how it's mine? You see how I try
to wake up?
*The horse whose neck is clothed with thunder—*
They were good ones.

I am the only one here, a giant,
asleep on the floor.

I am on the floor
of my invention, my forest
of dark sayings—
*The Lord shall hiss.*

My forest is always the same.
I am asleep on the damp floor.

My lids are down. Your face is a secret.
*Hiss, hiss.*

## Duressor

In darkness, crabs are believed to rest.
It is nobody's world. It is even less
theirs when they touch that first
inch of beach and the stunning blow
of elastic fire that is nobody's star
knocks them out of existence,
knocking them out like knees
in a murderous arena of tungsten lamps
and questioners. Of tables and pounding
fists. Of the decision of tide
to rebel against attraction, flattening out,
the moon looking up in surprise
from the underside of the stagnant water,
twisted and sad, like a coroner's eye
scrambled in a dearth of time,
the faraway body's insomnia, the crabs
combing the sand without minds.

## Solar Wind

I don't pray.
I just walk out there
where it's thin
with my bow and aim.

But I should have yelled.
I should have changed the world.

A person can die of balance,
just gleam like squid
and disappear.

The fence around our house
is soft with rain.
It can't stop my arrows.
It can't stop

what wants to happen,
the meteors I hear, power lines
blowing from the mountain,

or the girl somewhere
who reads you,
whose skin has memorized your life.
Nothing stops her fingers;
they swim with you at night.

Leave if you're leaving.
Leave plain mud.

I don't know what else
is on your beard.
It would be mercy, God.

I grow weird in the field.

## Benefits of Drowning

The light has been so awful.
Not whipped as a child,
I'm scared of human power.
They say there is an end
but I go round and round
with unscrupulous desires
in regions of my throat.
Nests smell from neglect.
Autumn will smell too
if the summer wasn't good.
Hard rain brings exaltation.
All the little mouths come out,
blowing rings of brightness.
I can enter them, not stagger,
not a skeleton, not plagued,
not by ghosts.

## Koan

You cross a broken field.
*Mirror, mirror.*
There's a scarecrow in a dress.

Sometimes I know
I won't see you again.
It's a bad place

to get emotional, alone
in the car, haze pouring
through the valley.

But I see you on your knees,
I see everything,
her stick arms pull you

to her skirt, hens
seeking shelter, I hear
crying. I hear crying

as the only true noise,
a chorus of tearing ice,
the dead straw

she is made of
crying, crows caught
in the sky, a duct

of her odd world;
in your rush to get in,
you bruise the shape

of your being.
This window I look out of
traps my breath

until nothing I pound
isn't part mine,
and black-and-blue inside.

## Eel

Then I will rest,
long, in a freeze, falling
through the life of the lake, long,
like heartbreak, long
through the element of coma,
a world of no enemies, no friends,
like an eye that won't open,
that grows long out of nowhere to look
and becomes its own place,
falling through blindness,
like a beam from the time of stars
whose death meant arrival,
and then I don't know
if I'm all that the water knew
or water is all I was,
if falling is falling backwards,
falling out of love,
like sound falling back into silence
as if swallowed by bog,
a bog that hangs in the balance
before swallowing God.

# II.

## One Thousand Bullfrogs Rejoice

It is dark inside the body, and wet,
and double-hearted. There are so many ways
to go, and not see, and lose
the feeling of the thread, which was alleged
to be invisible, and lose the man,
the fast Athenian, to someone with less rootage,
and never reach the fabled center,
afraid that if you did, you would find the hybrid,
not the hero, beautiful.

If you want to jump ahead,
Chapter Two just tells you how you erred
in Chapter One, taking his hand first
and being honest. Chapter Three says never mind,
you won't get another chance
to guide him. No one loves a volunteer.
No one loves a savior.
Chapter Four is set along the shore
where you are hiding, where life outside you
changes surface hourly.
Chapter Five: a skeleton is tangled
in a hyacinth. Their intimate clutch,
only for a minute, weirds you.
Tide is always bringing those reminders.
But here you keep in tune with rhythmic raging.
You open like a mussel made of gold
to anything in want of shelter,
anything with devious or laudable intentions.
Chapter Six. You open like a song
and bellow in the ear of second guessing.

## Leaving the Eccentric

The queenfish visits the spring
every spring, and she does it alone,
carried away from her silvery coast,
the blue drum region, carried away
by the aerial ocean above,
the dipping and rising, sidling along
saddles of thawing mountains,
thrashing through caribou tracks,
past dens of bears, exposing herself
to countless dangers, because of a whim
to be in the iciest possible
water, up to her eyes in the highest
spring, spring on the fringe of fish
civilization, spring where the king,
who loves her, lives, year after year,
for this single visit, the look of pain
on his outer face as he remembers
he should eat her. That's when the queen
takes her leave, flapping her battered
tail, slipping her body under. That's when
the one who loves her screams,
sharding the spring with manic octaves
(like bells of mules setting hills
ringing with each beating)—what else
can they do but follow its law
in wonder, the law of the sun
which burns, pulling the world to it,
the paradox of equinox, when light
and dark, and less and great, are all
the same, and every answer

strings its question up in space:
are blood and love just things that run,
and if they're not, do they belong
to what they are, or to the place
they're running to or from, and what
if that's the point of life, to turn
your back into your front
and mount the beast again?

## Isolato

The ox is slow but the earth is patient.
The ox is in a war
of many tiers but no engagement,
like folds within a bellows
that broke from the accordion
(war to be alone in a shiftless wind
that does not answer,
war to be the only
child in existence, even frozen,
be the only sound that plows the only land,
and as the only one,
be dumb to all remembrance
of how small or strong or round
it ever was, how much work there is
undone, how long it's been
since any form of water has come down,
all thought about the whip,
how sharp it is against the moving bone,
all gone).
The earth is patient in this war,
knowing binds and chains
enflame the skin, and skin, like soft terrain,
loosens into freedom for the thorn,
and the thorn, squeezing from the tissue
like a devil or a leech,
bleeds into an almost touching song.

## Givers and Takers

Father from afar,
where you have touched her,
you are not:

almost a gush
as she opens up, famously loud,
inhaling the sky

and seminal dust
and man-made fly. Almost a gush
as you reel her out

and drop her on a pile.
One is a giver,
another a taker, life of fire.

Now your fingers,
quickly skillful, chop her up;
can't they tell her

from the captured,
lying stiffly on a platter,
torsos only,

grilled and blackened?
Wherever her mind is
(with the gutstuff, in the bucket,

floating homeward
without bonework), it's losing
focus, kindling inward,

winding down.
Trees ripple through her
severed fantail; aurora shadows

flail each eye.
Aren't you tickled, father, tackler,
to find her still alive,

find her bobbing,
like a fraction, top by bottom,
multiplied? Almost a gush

as partial daughter
loiters on the waist-high water,
flirting, gurgling,

words like tinsel,
*Take me with you, I forgive you—*
final shimmer, final bite.

# Homogeny

There are light and milk and worship
on us all, which is why
I don't mind if she's spotted.
Hills are just plains
that rose in disobedience,
*how long can you hold your anger,*
blanched with latent purity,
bowed back down,
the way breasts ask forgiveness of the body
for being supernatant,
cowering, when all the mouths are done.
Twins are the way
love fell through me twice,
so I fix them to her udder
like slow-chewing fire. Which is why
I don't mind. Go,
if you're furious with women.
Go and do some rising. Milk is the proof
that what we disturb
in turn disturbs beautifully,
clearing the moon like a ruminant martyr.

## Meteor

I chose this. To be this
stone, grow nothing. I wanted this
absolute position in the heavens
more than anything, than you,
my two, too beautiful, my children.
A man I knew once
muttered in his terrors of the night,
*no, no, no,* instead of yelling.
It was this, this dismal low,
that made me leave him. I will leave them.
All the butterflies the lord above
can muster, all their roses.
I will leave whatever colors
struggle to be noticed. To leave,
to leave, that's the verb I am,
have always been, always will be,
heading, like a dewdrop,
into steamy confrontation,
my train of neural green
lasting half a second
before casting off its freight—his arms
outside the sheet, how warm they were,
like Rome the year it burned,
Nero at the window, loving no one,
fusion crust. I fly because
my space is crossed
with fear and hair and tail and hate,
the bowels of a lioness,
iron in her roar.

## Elsewhere

Did you hear, *I heard*,
that I flew, *you flew*,
at dusk, like the foxes,
my eyes, *your eyes*,
silver-white, like foxes,
and flew, *you flew*,
over things, *what things*,
in there, *in where*,
the trees, *what trees*,
reached up, *reached what*,
for me, my fur,
*your fur, I heard*,
they pulled, *pulled what*,
our love, *a ruse*,
was rare, on earth,
like stars that fall,
*like ice*, and spread,
*spread what*, my legs,
*your legs*, were white,
*silver-white, like ice*,
and shook, *shook what*,
my heart, *what heart*,
in truth, our love,
*a ruse*, on earth,
was caught, *by what*,
by things, *what things*,
my tongue, *your tongue*,
was white, *silver-white*,
like leaves, and split,
*split what*, in two,

*like ghosts*, at dusk,
like wings, *they whisht*,
not hurt, in truth,
just lost, *a ruse*.

## Deer Crossing the Sea

Many things were like sleep,
wholly in the power of the forest,
the deep middle, deep shiver, deep shade,
from which many things ran, unawake,
in search of new mountains to graze,
covered in flowers, *my love, I am sick*,
or covered in snow, pink with algae,
in search of impossible light
made of water, whose sapphire waves
swathed their heads, *you were only a dream*,
as they swam out to meet it, kicking their hooves,
no longer breathing, because no one
or nothing can quit once the body gets wind
of an eden—the promise of nectar
haunts them forever, the shore pecked out
of their eyes, and there, in its stead,
something greater to catch,
a scent that would paralyze God.

# III.

# [Argument]

*Od is a mineral kingdom. Anoton suspects his mother of breaking the law against harboring plants and animals. He reports her; she is demolished. Anoton's father takes revenge. The boy's head falls to Earth and becomes a small mountain island. Millennia later, a girl washes up on it. With the aid of a dog, Anoton devours her.*

# Boulders

He knew she was hiding a bee. He could hear it
zapping inside her, trapped in the amber
nook that led to her mineral uterus.

He had been born with that sound,
the rain of maracas, maraud of a rose, and so lived
in his mind with a wax city, silver hives

of see-through honey, chambers crammed
with princess-waste and ice, and would be
almost crazy, brushing her outer stone,

of which he had grown enamored,
like a pilot of a bombsite, fingering the lever—
this century wants anything. Is that a soul?

# Idol

Her organs were the resins of ancient pines,
rich with seeds and loess, fatal powders
of a lunatic faust, now-diseased meadows.
Anoton spilled the secret—wouldn't we all
to get what we want? He told the king
of her whewellite eyes, siliceous oozes,
horn-mad noises in her pelvic forest.
The king had her crushed, the loot handed
over in a moonstone box. But no matter how
hard Anoton shook, the bee was a silent
guest, a pressure point, a foil, a defiant sponge
that shrivels up in spite of what supplies it.

## Pornography

Her rubble was displayed in the royal
courtyard in cases labeled animal
and vegetable-corrupted. Her brain,
in a flask of boric acid, zithered the air
like luciferin, a glowing warning.

When Anoton came, he sized her up
with equal parts of severed feeling,
relieved to note her mental dwindling.
Then out she went—in clouds of white.
It was his first and finest blanket.

## Reaper

His father stepped out in full obsidian splendor
and swung. “Papa!” The head flew off
like a petrified stork, up through the roofless
house and out of the belt of metallic cloud
that kept the stone race bound, and flew
like liberation through the cold infinitude
that expands inside the living like a cache
of eggs. Does it matter what we’re made of?
A grain unfolds, the sun, the same, making
gold of morning. The facts then change: gold
is bad, the sun is pain, the malt, black rot—
and all that faith gets cut from our first story.

# Ignoramus

We are held to death like the knife
to the objective, mistaking the objective,
ever missing, except once. Anoton
was just a boy, and just his head—giant clod
of blistered jade—was falling fast to Earth
with the loud whist of a gas flame
colliding with a liquid proof. Eternal life
is nonsense. We who are old and full of words
consent to disappear. Anoton did not.
He hit the base of an unfished sky and lay,
a numb grenade, gummed with strombs
whose stomachs pulsed and slavered.

## Passive-Aggressive Music

Crests breaking over his severed neck
dumped salt on his lips and the salt
formed cakes like infected sores.
In time, the cakes became domes,
and gulls set their nests in the dome
umbrellas. But during the midday
summer sun, even the shade there
shone, like Judas' eyes on the fish
at supper. He never wondered where
his body was. He only murmured
to the gull who seemed to know him
something about his mother's pitch,
the sharp injustice of its softness,
and what's so important that it makes
you forget, like ammonia, everything?

## Naves and Navels

The sea is the greatest mother.
Even now that we know she is finite and dirty,
we still come back to her rim, admitting
we still belong there, like those to the church
when it's time to be joyfully married,
assured by an airtight seal.

The night the girl was hurled
onto the mountain, the sky was a pulverized
rose. There were walls in the air,
pink, trembling spires. Did Anoton know?
Does anyone know? We who are old
and full of words?

The gardens of Od had no flowers. Call it
the spell of perfume. It takes the wind
of our breath to float a paper boat,
and the damage that follows is real. "The king
has long ears; the king has long ears."
It echoes. We know.

## Weavers

In the late afternoon when the thrust
of the waves turns violet,
Anoton's violets wave. That's how the shade

of her hair is decided.
That her eyes are pins of stars
he is told by the gull—

because he has to know, has to ask,
because the place in his ear
where she lies is phonolithic

and the sound that it makes when her body
stirs jolts him like existence.
He tries to shy away, but can't raise his head

from the ocean bottom. Can you weave
if you are woven?
Can you drown if you are stone?

Is wind your only supper?
Does it scarf your mouth, loud with wolf.
or hem-and-haw, like maidenhood?

## Accessory

Things breed in the bath
of Anoton's mouth the world
has never seen: worms with plumes,
newt-like ghouls, armadillo
boas. As the gull describes the girl
over and over, his floor grows warm
with flaming sugar. Can we
avoid the misadventure?
Is it seductive to obey?

The gull, whose name is Mara,
swoops without warning and pulls a tuft
of the sleeping girl's hair.

The girl doesn't cry, only probes the spot
in a state of wonder. The skins
of the moon are exposed when we behold it;
we call the bloodless bruises *seas*.
Falling apart is like going undercover—
we drop our sunny side
to meet the dirt,

then loiter there, eyelids halfway
closed, no longer certain
if the disarray down our face
and neck is ours or theirs.

## Stalactite Habit

Mara drags the hair across Anoton's lips for hours.
The hair swishes. His surface
ripples like the all-knowing muscle of a horse.

He asks to feel it in his throat.
Noodles of drool
coil on the topaz water. Balanced on a tooth

formation, mid-mouth down, Mara drops it.
He asks for more. Mara pauses. He asks for more
These are the hesitations

that make us who we are, mark us for the haul:
*No*, the oldest word in the vainest circle.
*Yes*, the promise that burns,

mathematically tapers, banks on its slick
like biblical siblings:
*Yes, we will serve you, and mock*

*the just sun. Yes, we will put*
*our trust in your shadow. Yes, yes,*
*and dress all your longings, and relish your bite.*

## S.O.S

The girl was scooping clams
when the gull pulled a switchblade
lunge. Instead of hair,
the beak took a cube of flesh.

Mara shut her eyes,
flew dutifully back, the catch more akin
to a cherry. Why is the worst
the only certainty?

Anoton didn't thank her,
just sucked and sucked
until it must have changed from red
to paraffin by morning.

The sweet rubber of everything.
Why did Mara do it,
appoint her home her master?
We are orphans. We have never

had a father in the sky.
The earth and the water will leave us,
but oxygen first, and away
like a gasp went Mara,

mean as the arrow
her soul had become, deserting her young
to yell unto no one.
We must get out of this infancy.

It isn't erotic. The smile no longer
moves us, only the loathing,
and that by itself
makes a dangerous papoose.

## Transubstantiation

Anoton gave orders.
The mutt of history listened,
or whatever it was, monarchy's
harpy, then bounded down the cliff
on cloven fours.

When it reached the beach,
the girl was leaning on a shoulder.
(As soon as he had stabbed her,
Achilles raped her—Penthesilea, the soldier,
lifeless in her breastplate.)

Smoke is *lacrimosus*.
In smoke and in tears, ecstasy
bristles, like the paunch of an ostrich
under a livid sword.

When the dog bared its teeth,
froth breaking forth,
the shoulder vanished. It must have been
an angel's. A human would have
stayed, at least to seem to save her.

## Pecuniary

It seized her by the waist
and ran, her dangling head
bashing the rocks,

the rocks bashing back.
At the top, abrupt silence—
like a dropped baton.

What better rush
than an urge served fresh,
the girl's brief worth

scrolled up tight, a Persian rug,
the blood at rest,
a pervert's inertial toy?

What does a whippet imagine?
What could a trophy
mean to an Arabian?

We love this preposterous
quest. When it nudges her
into the pit, her body clinks,

an exhausted bauble,
rolls down the walls
of the buyer's yawn,

his wholesale gulp,
her edible cunt,
an optimum bargain.

## Victorious Female

Victorious how? Anoton's
mind grows spastic.
Olive trees snarl the hill.

rams with curved horns
batter each other, deranged
by bubbling groins.

Sperm splashes the pampas,
mist of aborted rainbows.
Just to exist is criminal.

His breezes go cyclone,
coastlines discordant as ever.
He longs for permanent

burial. *Where is my therapy?*
Schism, fulfillment.
He's Venus's son:

he stomachs her love,
vomits her silver pajamas
and goblets. It cannot

be tallied, this theatre
of war. She tweets
every morning, unhinges

her box, offers him
oranges, puddings, abalone
guns that don’t cock.

## Dark Eros

She smirks, sets herself up
on a cinder cone—How does
it feel, she asks the old mountain,
to have no choice but to feel?
Succuss of Anoton's glottis.
Rumbles, plutonic debris.
Feel this, she hisses into his
sphincter, then does something
evil with fruit—oh, the power
to cry! Oh, to be able to cry!
His mouth is under the sea now.
The past is a quasi-fetish.
I was only a child, but my
obsession with you was divine.

## I, Anoton

I in the torso
lying on the floor
with my mourning
dad. I in the finding
that I am not restricted
to my lithic head.
I in the vulture
who shrugs off the future,
I in the wide
open field of reform.
I in the gnome
alone on the seesaw,
always the low end,
squatter for hope.
I and my birdie
bride in a furrow
of a burnt winter coat
of a nobody soldier.
I in my carriage,
immaculate newborn,
safe from the knowledge
that I would expand
in poundage and
damage, that mother
could shift from
comforting lifter
to object to possibly
terribly conquer—
I in the useless
sorry that haunts me

like a napkin of snow
laundered in April,
caught by the water
as if by an eyeball,
an intimate witness
to thin-skinned nature.
Who would believe
such a fancy flirtation,
such feathery radii,
could leave any imprint?
A boy made of stone
is harder to pardon.
So why do you bother,
father, to hold my
cold body and cry?

# IV.

## Circling Disease

The sum of things is the least of things.
The dwarf loved the sovereign's
daughter repeatedly:

at first, every morning, then he added on
noon, then the army honed in
like a giant umbrella.

She was carried away like a dark subject
until all that she felt and could not say
hung like a nightworld spider.

*Omni et nullo*. Eggs in a multiplet
structure, increasingly plump;
mother at the apogee, legs glued shut.

## Fruit of Discord

Mine is a dry tree.
The sons of aliens want me.
They have a need. We all
have a need. To construct
a man made of grass
is the grass widow's need,
but she lies in the heat
of the wet tilled field,
unfulfilled, rewriting her
need. If heaven were bigger,
if hell less a machine–
are they beaming at me?
Are they singing? Someone
needs honey, someone else
cream or foam, another
needs Helen, a raw eleven,
barechested, hurling
stones. What is your need?
Not me? Not my worm?
Not to love what is worn?
Not to lick my sick peels
but to ram her hard breath
in the gym? Whose side
are you on? If you want
something quick, but need it
to last, a manifest tryst,
no strings attached, pick me.
My hole is black.

## Mangiafuoco

Now picture this—me, your wife,
a snail. Picture my insular freedom.
It snows and no one sees me
at home in my own white shoulder.

Pulcinella, Arlecchino,
beating each other with sticks;
your overly merry music
ripping through space like ice—

*The Grand Puppet Theatre!*
Already far from spite,
the caravan, our wooden children
strapped inside, I kissed them all

goodbye, your ruby lantern eyes
blackening behind me. Divorce.
Beard from head to floor,
whip made of fox and snake…

What would I be
if I hadn't been pitted against you?
My soul would have no furniture
to burn on a night like this.

## Ladybirds

Brilliance is a carcass
on a snow-white beach.

Envy never sleeps.
I tell my children truthfully:

a long red beard is breaking
from the darkness scale.

He's chasing you because
you're new. Because he's old

and sees the town in dirty tones:
violet sheep and wine-dark

corn. He burns the evening
rainbow like a war-time bridge

until it's charred and charlatans
topple out of robin eggs

and pox your happy window
by capturing the ledge—

chattering like x-rays
that crash into your flesh.

## Sunflower

Wind takes your hair
like a hooligan owl
and leaves a deep pocket
of dusk in your scalp.

Love without pride
is a love with no end.
You keep calling me in
to fill up your head,

but the mutinous dust
of the dead yellow field
says better not listen
to a thing with a stem.

## Windmill

I can't cry so I
smack the extent
of my face but I
can't so I hate
the oblique of my
vanes but with hate
I can whish any
bird into gore, abort
any fate, con wind
to kill corn. I wear
a wood kilt. I stand
straight but my head
makes the rounds
of a whore who is
more or less doomed
to feel less and do
more. Sometimes
I pause in an unforeseen
calm. I don't care
what I am. It's drama
I farm, making meal
out of drear by dragging
it on—with arms that
would harrow the hair
on a groin, I man
the horizon, I garland
the void, I castrate
the sun and the gang
of vague air that used to
support me but warped

my career, so I turn
without mercy, I burn
my goodwill,
like a snail on a purge
who takes the bran in
and breaks the bran down—
a sanitized foot
on tour in the dung.

## Water Bears

We, pawing the edges
of our water-cage
where everything internal
stops. Where the colorless
jello of our unlaunched
bellies sends ripples
to the water's top—in this,
this hideous transparency,
we languish,
our child heads held under
by your polar mother hands.
It didn't have to be like this.
There was light in the world, too,
choice in the game of chance:
the teeny-tiny cyclops
drags her bags of eggs,
slave to microbial angst.
But the brain laid bare to Satan
was also home to laughs—
*Mom, give an eye to God.*
*The five of us have forty legs.*
*In the afterlife,*
*the clowning never ends.*

## Tantalus Gossips

She rose, I hear, from hell again,
and rummaged through the river,

grabbed it by its bleeding stem,
shoved it up her private—

Orpheus's singing head
still bringing her to climax.

Love and death, they never quit.
What a gruesome couple to behold.

I'd rather be alone in want
than be between her legs,

beheaded. Rather neck
the airy waif of punishment

than hump the skull
of puppy love remembered.

## Rooster's Greeting

*Cock-a-doodle doo*
*the dirty girl is here anew.*

She comes with a light
touch of the whip
and all of her love
outstretched        as if
nymphomania could save her

a rising and falling
acrobat
as was made her
by her father
with all of his love
outstretched        as if

comes like a whip

not looking for him
but *him*
who doesn't love her

who does succor
in the forest
almost as stoic
as Christ
and far more virile

and it needs to go deep
through the neck
of the womb and it does

because she is the sun
and breathes on his sperm

and he does

because she is the sun
and no one
can't love her

## Claw Asteroid

The soul is a tyrant.
The soul is a child.
Heartless, eyeless,

roundish sponge
in mindless fornication
with the ocean.

Then comes daylight.
Lovers leave
in tiny spaceships.

Good times drying
up in gallons.
Check your finder:

it won't come back,
the moist embrace.
You don't live anywhere now

you can't imagine.
That's why you shoot
at close range.

## Virginals

Marigolds close
before storms.

Some mammals, too,
in the too-stillness,

pull in their radar,
bend over.

Here, where no ceiling
on earth

has ever been so high
as here,

is the man
who loves virginals

swinging his boy
into the storm

in his soul
and over the limits

of God
to be finished—

drained of the face
that is too much whore's

becoming angel's
being finished.

## Trance Logic

Robbers love clouds.
Clouds cloud their heads
like breasts.

Thick love serves
both ends.

Clouds love theft—
the ivory combs
in Cathy's hair,
the purse's breath.

Awareness is a cup.
You can raise it to the heavens,
yell for everyone to come.

They won't feel
the lake of knives
they have to cross,
if thought is safe,

or know the raw grenade
of unexploited beauty
going off
a mind away.

They come as thought
and thought is safe.
In fields of gold
and blue-gold grapes,
they take your cup
and self-erase.

## Dinnerbird

we are so far inward
we no longer hear
the snow

solitude's eggs
fill the air

because the depths
must be limited
must know there are ends

we send music-box daughter
a poisoned arrow
and wait for the hole
in her chest

hole after hole
in the grouse-sucked dark
of the bird-worm's home

where a table is set
for god knows what
must have kindled terror
in the place of love

and still no way into her heart
to let her know
the beast will have his piece
of juvenile red

and rise when he is done with it
and maybe then

## Murder-Music

You can't
fake a calling,

Carlo
Gesualdo.

You were called
to make madrigals,

then called on
to kill,

then you called
back the sinners

by painting them
here—in the convent

Capuchin—
to what?

Feel called on
some more?

Kill them again?
Make more and more

madrigals,
again and again?

We can't really see them,
naked, burning,

below and behind
the crumbling altar,

yet we know,
Carlo Gesualdo,

Prince of Venosa,
there is no better music

than morally
unknowable, morally

unownable,
morally killable

organs and holes
we can't really see

but feel
through the syllable.

## Frost

Wild dogs are at home
in their trysts
with the dream-shapes
Sometimes a puff is enough

for the sea-going canoe
to be available
to climb into and get over
the byss of abyss with

and ride for as long as it takes
Jesus to sleep
and come out of it warm
like from something illicit

like knees that move of themselves
on the pilgrimage
to see the last horrible apple
drop from the maiden tree

## Surrender to the Maid

Only a fool goes here
and there.

The owl stays,
accumulates eyes

by staying.
The trousers stay,

the virgin-pubis,
the king's betrayal.

Tomorrow stays.
The jailer's breath

rains on Joan,
a ghoul's champagne.

Odium,
the true redeemer,

anxious enough
in its gnat's-breath time

to rip the dungeon open,
stays.

And Michael, and Anna,
and Catherine,

Lucy,
bidding on Joan,

all of them,
saints,

and the man
whose divinity nailed her

to Him,
and his nails,

they're all here.
They all stay.

# V.

## Farm before Time

A stone can be told
to soften. Soft,
it will flatten, darken.
Soft, it might hang itself
up in the trees
or grow gills
and sparkle with poison.
You can tell it to cry,
kneel at your boots,
let down some milk,
whatever your mood is.
But there in the trenches,
a stone comes to mind
as the soul that went soft
in ways it could hide.

## L-Field

The world is embryonic.
Wolf doesn't see her face,
only the forehead,
tiara-ed,
pulling his yearning
through the ten-thousand trees
like thread.

Girl doesn't feel
the jerk of his limbs,
only the waves,
how to measure the waves
that congeal like winter blood,
and fend off the filth
of enemy-breath, and build
cocoon enough—

How dead does she have to be
to be left in the life-field
with just enough life
not to be?

It was her name
scratched in the dirt
with a nail.
It was her name—
how not to go out like a light
in the abattoir
but to surge through the pain
with a wholly bright shape,

make temple of template,
sacred of sake,
egg of the ghost-stuff,
ghost of the egg.

## Abel

Unable to say what it is
that doesn't sit well.

It sits in the dark like a smile
that doesn't sit well.

Like a boy made of straw
who quietly tears his stomach out

as soon as he tucks it in.
Day like an empty breast.

Night like a shivering tent
that sits on the face like a crepe

over undefined bone.
Like a childhood phantom

that lives in the floor like a wave,
curls up like a lip that won't say—

if rot is at halt in the throat,
if time slides away, if witness

is rust and silence is blanket,
then why does the horse want to kiss?

Why does the air smell like Cain?

## Peacock Mosaic

Hermit lives
on herbs, dew,
mystery.

Hermit keeps
peppercorn eyes
on all that passes

because all that passes
rolls right off
the trusted shoulder,

like drops off water
briefly feathered
by the wind of death,

that, briefly feathered,
never feel
the ground they never left.

## Remanence

Ogres make love in the open,
then bury the parts.

If you listen,
you can almost find them:

a moan, then two,
in the oil-drum

where tender filigrees of stone
bind them down.

Just one splash
can redirect the mind:

Paul on the road to Damascus
kept turning around,

heard water where there wasn't,
heard earth remember

where there was—
do you know how much that hurts?

Being puzzled back together
from a blast?

Riding the marsh-horse
where the marsh is all sponge

and the feeling is love
until the whale with strange breath

blows into your dream-ear,
where it was.

## Moss

Godawful sleeping father
forgets that we, too, are asleep
and cannot know the cause of it—
who the creatures were
who amassed at father's brow,
brandishing torches,
cannot know if they were made
aware, while burning, too,
that darkness can't be vanquished,
only battered, dispersed
like molecules of fear,
like what we have for shrines now,
these streams of fertile hair
that wrap the eyes in lost desire
to be anywhere but here.

## Yam House

the heart is counterfeit
and often faraway

i don't walk or sail
to get there

i close my eyes
and pile up

like bright green stuffing
and that's how i know

this heavenly thing
that was taken from me

that's how i know
it was stabbed

where the love was
where the vampire grazes

as if he could taste us
deep in the earth

with our clothes on
as if we were acorns

or paralyzed mice
lying in wait

like a memorized knife
in a daydream

## Triple Crime

Magic has a deadline.
It's late for the sea-cow,
yet here she still is
in her soft depression,
in the skin of a newborn,
a face like spring,
though her era is dead and gone.
It's late for the sea-cow,
but she's sticking around,
eager for the sons of Cain
to kneel at her side,
mistake her for mermaid,
open their homes to her charm.

But the sons of Cain
aren't going to make it.
They took the bad road.
They know all they know.
The womb will forget them;
pomp is brought down
to the grave. Yet
they still ride the wheel,
imbibing the air
of the netherworld chamber
where the girl on fire
is pregnant with fire,
the magical ransom met.

## ACKNOWLEDGMENTS

"Sanctuary," "Ignis Fatuus," "Flight of the Mice," "Radiolaria," "Io Remembers," "Holy Ghost," "Duressor," "Solar Wind," "Benefits of Drowning," "Koan," and "Eel" from *Dark Sky Question*, Copyright © 1998 Larissa Szporluk. Reprinted with permission of Beacon Press, Boston.

"One Thousand Bullfrogs Rejoice," "Leaving the Eccentric," "Isolato," "Givers and Takers," "Homogeny," "Meteor," "Elsewhere," and "Deer Crossing the Sea" from *Isolato,* Copyright © 2000 Larissa Szporluk. Reprinted with permission of the University of Iowa Press.

"[Argument]," "Boulders," "Idol," "Pornography," "Reaper," "Ignoramus," "Passive-Aggressive Music," "Naves and Navels," "Weavers," "Accessory," "Stalactite," "Habit," "S.O.S," "Transubstantiation," "Pecuniary," "Victorious Female," "Dark Eros," and "I, Anoton" from *Embryos & Idiots*, Copyright © 2000 Larissa Szporluk. Reprinted with permission of Tupelo Press. All rights reserved.

"Circling Disease," "Fruit of Discord," and "Mangiafuoco" from *The Wind, Master Cherry, the Wind*. Copyright © 2003 Larissa Szporluk. Reprinted with the permission of The Permissions Company, LLC on behalf of Alice James Books, alicejamesbooks.org. All rights reserved.

"Ladybirds," "Sunflower," "Windmill," "Water Bears," and "Tantalus Gossips" from *Traffic with Macbeth*, Copyright © 2011 Larissa Szporluk. Reprinted with permission of Tupelo Press. All rights reserved.

"Rooster's Greeting," "Claw Asteroid," "Virginals," "Trance Logic," "Dinnerbird," "Murder-Music," "Frost," and "Surrender to the Maid" from *Virginals*, Copyright © 2021 Larissa Szporluk. Reprinted with permission of Burnside Review Press.

LARISSA SZPORLUK is the author of six books of poetry, including *Dark Sky Question*, winner of the Barnard Prize, *Isolato* (Iowa Book Prize), and *Virginals*, which won the Burnside Review Press Prize. She is the recipient of a Guggenheim Fellowship and National Endowment for the Arts grant, and received graduate degrees from the University of California at Berkeley and the University of Virginia. A former professor of poetry and ongoing mother of three, she now farms in northern Italy.

RECENT AND SELECTED TITLES FROM TUPELO PRESS

*Song in Tammuz*
AVIA TADMOR

*AutoPortrait (as flotsam)*
KIRSTEN KASCHOCK

*Other Paths for Shahrazad*
JENNIFER JEAN, ED.

*Them That Slept*
LARISSA SZPORLUK

*Slipstream*
DIANA CAO

*The Book of Marys and Glaciers*
CARRIE OLIVIA ADAMS

*The Andrew Wyeth Chronicles*
JANÉE BAUGHER

*Identifying the Pathogen*
JENNIFER MILITELLO

*Indifferent Cities*
ÁNGEL GARCÍA

*Something Small of How to See a River*
TERESA DZIEGLEWICZ

*Force Drift: An Essay in the Epic*
JEFFREY PETHYBRIDGE

*Tips to Help You Do Your Best*
MIKE CARLSON

*Cyborg Fever*
LAURIE SHECK

*Daphne*
KRISTEN CASE

*Nebulous Vertigo*
BELLE LING

*Westminster West*
CHARD DE NIORD

*Jalousie*
ALLYSON PATY

*Mycocosmic*
LESLEY WHEELER

*Phantom Number: An Abecedarium for April*
SPRING ULMER

*The Haunting*
CATE PEEBLES

*The Radiant*
LISE GOETT

*The Opening Ritual*
G.C. WALDREP

*The Right Hand*
CHRISTINA PUGH

*Called Back*
ROSA LANE

*Landsickness*
LEIGH LUCAS

*Green Island*
LIZ COUNTRYMAN

*The Beautiful Immunity*
KAREN AN-HWEI LEE

*Small Altars*
JUSTIN GARDINER

*Country Songs for Alice*
EMMA BINDER

*Asterism*
AE HEE LEE

*then telling be the antidote*
XIAO YUE SHAN

*Therapon*
BRUCE BOND & DAN BEACHY-QUICK

*membery*
PREETI KAUR RAJPAL

*How To Live*
KELLE GROOM

*Sleep Tight Satellite*
CAROL GUESS

*THINE*
KATE PARTRIDGE

*The Future Will Call You Something Else*
NATASHA SAJÉ

*Night Logic*
MATTHEW GELLMAN

*The Unreal City*
MIKE LALA

*Wind—Mountain—Oak: Poems of Sappho*
DAN BEACHY-QUICK

*Tender Machines*
J. MAE BARIZO

*Best of Tupelo Quarterly*
KRISTINA MARIE DARLING, ED.

*We Are Changed to Deer at the Broken Place*
KELLY WEBER

*Why Misread a Cloud*
EMILY CARLSON

*The Strings Are Lightning and Hold You In*
CHEE BROSSY

*Ore Choir: The Lava on Iceland*
KATY DIDDEN AND KEVIN TSANG

*The Air in the Air Behind It*
BRANDON RUSHTON

*The Future Perfect: A Fugue*
ERIC PANKEY

*American Massif*
NICHOLAS REGIACORTE

*City Scattered*
TYLER MILLS